TOP 10 BASEBALL PITCHERS

Michael J. Sullivan

SPORTS TOP 10

ENSLOW PUBLISHERS, INC.

44 Fadem Rd.   P.O. Box 38

Box 699   Aldershot

Springfield, N.J. 07081   Hants GU12 6BP

U.S.A.   U.K.

Library of Congress Cataloging-in-Publication Data

Sullivan, Michael John, 1960–
   Top 10 baseball pitchers / by Michael J. Sullivan.
      p. cm.—(Sports top 10)
   Includes bibliographical references (p.) and index.
   ISBN 0-89490-520-1
    1. Pitchers (Baseball)—United States—Biography—Juvenile
literature. [1. Baseball players. 2. Pitchers (Baseball)]
I. Title. II. Title: Top 10 baseball pitchers. III. Series.
GV865.A1S88 1994
796.357'22'0922—dc20
  [B]   94-2157
                 CIP
                 AC

Printed in the United States of America

10 9 8 7 6 5 4 3 2

Photo Credits: AP/Wide World Photos, pp. 11, 13, 15, 17; Los Angeles Dodgers, pp.
22, 25; National Baseball Library & Archive, Cooperstown, N.Y., pp. 7, 9, 19, 21, 26, 29,
30, 33, 42, 45; Michael Ponzini, pp. 34, 37, 41; Richard Raphael, pp. 39.

Cover Photo: AP/Wide World Photos.

Interior Design: Richard Stalzer.

CONTENTS

INTRODUCTION

A PITCHER IS THE MOST important player in the game of baseball. He affects the outcome of a ball game more than any other player. But to be a great pitcher you have to do more than throw a baseball at high speeds.

Yes, former Texas Ranger Nolan Ryan was a terrific pitcher because he had a great fastball. But Ryan won a lot of games because he could throw more than a fastball. Most hitters thought they would be able to see Ryan's fastball. But, Ryan would fool them by throwing his curve ball instead. The element of surprise is a great weapon for a pitcher!

To be able to trick a batter is certainly a wonderful weapon but a great pitcher must also have "control" over his pitches. He has to be able to throw the ball over the plate so the hitter won't get on base with a walk. Christy Mathewson was a pitcher with great control. In fact, he once went sixty-eight innings without walking anyone!

Besides having control over his pitches, a great pitcher can't "fall behind" on a hitter. When a pitcher doesn't throw enough strikes to a hitter, he gives the batter an opportunity to choose a pitch he likes before swinging. If that happens, the pitcher will have a very hard time getting a batter out.

A great pitcher must also be able to think. If a hitter is a good fastball hitter, a pitcher must know that. Great pitchers are always studying the hitters around the league and learning their weak points. Hall of Famer Tom Seaver was one pitcher who always knew a batter's weakness. "Your thinking and discipline have a lot to do with making it," Seaver said. "There are plenty of pitchers with ability who're just ordinary."[1]

A great pitcher must also take risks. During the course of

a ball game, there comes a time when a pitcher must throw a fastball to a good fastball hitter. Sandy Koufax did that in the opening game of the 1963 World Series when he struck out the great fastball hitter Roger Maris. Koufax took a risk by throwing not one, but two fastballs to Maris. It worked!

Last, but not least, a great pitcher must have determination and heart. Grover Cleveland Alexander overcame epilepsy and double vision to become a great pitcher. A tired Bob Gibson overcame his fatigue when he pitched—and won—three games in the 1967 World Series.

We've searched every decade of baseball history to come up with *our* list of the ten greatest pitchers. But the list does not end here. There are so many more great pitchers. After you finish this book, take some time in your library to read about some more. You will be surprised to learn how many great pitchers there have been in the game of baseball!

CAREER STATISTICS

Pitcher	Wins	Losses	Games	Innings Pitched	Hits	Bases on Balls (Walks)	Strikeouts	Earned-Run Average
GROVER C. ALEXANDER	373	208	696	5,189.1	4,868	953	2,199	2.56
ROGER CLEMENS	192	111	383	2,776	2,359	856	2,590	3.06
BOB GIBSON	251	174	528	3,884.2	3,279	1,336	3,117	2.91
WALTER JOHNSON	416	279	801	5,923	4,921	1,355	3,508	2.17
SANDY KOUFAX	165	87	397	2,324.1	1,754	817	2,396	2.76
CHRISTY MATHEWSON	373	188	634	4,782	4,216	838	2,502	2.13
SATCHEL PAIGE	28	31	179	476	429	183	290	3.29
NOLAN RYAN	324	292	807	5,387	3,923	2,178	5,714	3.10
TOM SEAVER	311	205	656	4,782.2	3,971	1,390	3,640	2.86
CY YOUNG	511	316	906	7,354	7,092	1,219	2,800	2.63

GROVER C. ALEXANDER

IT WAS A PITCHER'S NIGHTMARE. Grover Cleveland Alexander was asked by St. Louis Cardinals manager Roger Hornsby to try and save Game 7 of the 1926 World Series against the powerful New York Yankees. In the middle of their lineup, the Yankees had "Murderers Row"—Babe Ruth, Lou Gehrig, and Tony Lazzeri.

Alexander had already won two games as a starting pitcher in the series. But this situation was different. Now he was coming out of the bullpen to pitch in relief. The bases were loaded in the seventh inning. Earle Combs was on third. Bob Meusel was on second. Gehrig was on first. The batter was Lazzeri, a fastball hitter. Alexander's first pitch was a curve. Lazzeri took a big swing. He missed! Alexander tried his fastball on the second pitch. Craacck! The ball went foul down the left field line.

Alexander was relieved. He wiped his forehead. He looked toward Lazzeri and took a quick peek at the runners. Then he threw his curve. Lazzeri swung . . . and missed! Strike three!

Alexander got the remaining six outs to help the Cardinals defeat the mighty Yankees for the Cardinals' first World Championship.

The pitcher's competitive instinct had been developed in battles with eleven brothers and sisters for a piece of food at the dinner table at the family farm in Elba, Nebraska. Alexander built up his strength and his arms by plowing corn in the field and working with mules on the farm. He developed his right arm and accuracy by throwing an ear of corn against an outlined spot on the side of the barn.

GROVER C. ALEXANDER

Grover Cleveland Alexander was named for Grover Cleveland, President of the United States, (1885–1889, 1893–1897). Most people just called him Alex.

Alexander overcame such health hazards as epilepsy and double vision. As a youngster, he was struck in the head by a thrown ball, almost ending his life. He was unconscious for two days before he recovered. Because of that injury, he had double vision for almost a year. Despite those hardships, Alexander continued to pitch.

Grover Alexander started out his major league career in 1911. In 1915, his 31–10 record led the Philadelphia Phillies to the World Series. Over the next two years, Alexander won thirty more games each season. Despite his success, Alexander was traded to the Chicago Cubs in 1918 where he remained until 1926.

Alexander is tied for third place for wins in the major leagues with 373. Christy Mathewson also had 373 wins. On the all-time major league shutout list, Alexander is second with 90 shutouts. On two occasions, he won two games on the same day!

His achievements were recognized in 1938 when he was elected to the National Baseball Hall of Fame. "I was never the worrying kind," Alexander said. "I always knew how to pitch. I wouldn't have pitched these many years in the major leagues if I did worry."[1]

GROVER C. ALEXANDER

BORN: February 26, 1887, Elba, Nebraska.

DIED: November 4, 1950, St. Paul, Nebraska.

PRO: Philadelphia Phillies, 1911–1917, 1930; Chicago Cubs, 1918–1926; St. Louis Cardinals, 1926–1929.

RECORDS: Pitched 16 shutouts in 1916. Second in Shutouts, 90.
Tied for third (with Christy Mathewson) in wins, 373.

HONORS: Elected to National Baseball Hall of Fame in 1938.

Alexander left major-league baseball to fight in World War I. He returned a changed man, alcoholic and permanently deafened by gunfire.

ROGER CLEMENS

"THE ROCKET" WAS LIVING UP to his nickname. Boston Red Sox pitcher Roger Clemens' fastball was exploding by the Seattle Mariners batters on April 29, 1986 at Boston's Fenway Park. Clemens was one strikeout away from tying a major-league record for strikeouts in a game. He had 18 and the crowd at Fenway was on its feet roaring at every strike.

Spike Owen, the Mariners shortstop, was the batter. Clemens threw his fastball. "Hisssss." The ball flew past Owen over the plate. "Strike one," the umpire tried to shout over the cheers of the Red Sox fans. Hissss! "Strike . . . ," The umpire's scream was drowned out by the roar. Clemens wasted no time. He spun towards the plate. Owen swung. He missed. Strike three! Could "The Rocket" break baseball's all-time record for strikeouts in a game? He sure was going to try!

Phil Bradley was the next batter. Clemens threw two straight fastballs past Bradley! The Boston fans were screaming as Clemens kicked his left leg high in the air and threw the ball. Strike three! Roger Clemens had set a new baseball record—20 strikeouts in a game. No other pitcher in baseball history has ever matched "The Rocket's" record.

Roger Clemens was born in Dayton, Ohio, on August 4, 1962. He played Little League ball and quickly gained a reputation as one of the best young players around. Later, Clemens was selected by the New York Mets right out of high school in June of 1981.

Roger turned down the Mets' offer and instead went to college. He helped lead the University of Texas to the College

ROGER CLEMENS

Roger Clemens is perhaps the greatest pitcher in baseball today. He set the league record for most strikeouts in a game, 20, in 1986.

World Series. That's where the legend of "The Rocket" started to form.

In 1983, Clemens was the nineteenth player chosen in the major-league draft. He was selected by the Red Sox. He pitched for a year in the minor leagues. Clemens posted a 9–4 rookie record and had to overcome a bad shoulder in 1985. But in 1986 "The Rocket" took off. Clemens led the Red Sox to the World Series. He had a 24–4 record and led the American League with a 2.48 ERA. He was second in strike-outs with 238. Roger Clemens was named the Most Valuable Player and was also honored with the Cy Young Award that year.

Clemens followed up this banner season by winning the Cy Young again, finishing with a 20–9 record. Clemens had eighteen complete games and seven shutouts; both led the American League. Clemens continued to win for the Red Sox. His 18–10 record in 1991 earned him his third Cy Young Award.

In 1992, Clemens finished third in the Cy Young ballot-ing. He had won eighteen games and lost eleven. He also remained consistent with his pitching that year. His ERA was lower in 1992 than the previous year—2.41. The following season did not go as well. Trying to fight off an injury to his right arm, Clemens had his worst season in the major leagues. He finished 11–14 with an ERA of 4.46. Despite his lack of success in 1993, though, there's no doubt that Clemens is one of baseball's greatest pitchers.

"This guy is going to be in the Hall of Fame someday," New York Yankees first baseman Don Mattingly said. "He's as good a pitcher as there is in baseball. You'll see him in Cooperstown someday. You can bet on it."[1]

ROGER CLEMENS

BORN: August 4, 1962, Dayton, Ohio.

COLLEGE: San Jacinto Junior College in Texas. University of Texas. Led Texas to NCAA championship in 1983.

PRO: Boston Red Sox, 1983– .

RECORDS: Set major-league record by striking out 20 batters in one game.

HONORS: Named MVP in 1986; Cy Young Award winner in 1986, 1987, 1991.

Clemens was honored with the Cy Young Award three times, 1986, 1987, and 1991.

Bob Gibson

It Was The Bottom Of the ninth inning in Game 7 of the 1967 World Series. Several million Americans were watching on television. Over thirty-five thousand Red Sox fans filled famous Fenway Park in Boston. On the mound was a very tired Bob Gibson for the St. Louis Cardinals. Gibson had already won two games in this series and he was working on his third. If he could complete the ninth inning, the Cardinals would win the World Series.

Despite Gibson being tired, St. Louis manager Red Schoendienst decided to keep Gibson in the game. The Cardinals were leading 7–2, but the Red Sox were a club that could score runs in a hurry. Carl Yastrzemski led off with a single and the Boston crowd roared. The next batter was Ken Harrelson. Gibson threw a slider and Harrelson grounded into a double play. The Red Sox fans were silent. Their last hope was George Scott.

Gibson and Scott battled back and forth. Now the count was 2–2. Scott fouled two pitches back. Gibson's next pitch was a high, inside slider. Scott swung and missed!

Bob Gibson had pulled off one of the greatest feats in the history of the World Series. He won three games, including the decisive last game. And he also homered in Game 7! It was no surprise that Gibson was named World Series MVP.

The ever-humble Gibson would say after the game: "I honestly believe [teammate] Lou Brock deserved it. Without him we couldn't have won. He was on base all the time and completely upset them with his running."[1]

Bob Gibson was born on November 9, 1935, in Omaha, Nebraska. Bob was one of seven children. His father died

BOB GIBSON

Bob Gibson led the St. Louis Cardinals to two World Series titles, in 1964 and 1967. Both times he was named series MVP.

three months before he was born. However, Bob's big brother Josh set him straight. Every day Josh would work with Bob on how to play baseball. He also taught Bob to be respectful and honest. Gibson was a great baseball player, but he also excelled in both basketball and track at Omaha Technical High School. Gibson eventually went to Creighton University. He played basketball with the Harlem Globetrotters in 1957. But baseball was his true love.

Gibson signed a professional baseball contract in 1957 and played thirteen games with St. Louis in 1959. It didn't take long for Gibson to establish himself as one of baseball's all-time great pitchers. He won 251 games in his career and finished with a 2.91 ERA. Gibson also struck out 3,117 batters. But he saved his best stuff for the World Series. He won seven games in three World Series. He also struck out a record seventeen Detroit Tigers in the 1968 World Series opening game.

In 1968, Gibson was recognized as the best player in the National League with the Most Valuable Player award. In addition, he won the Cy Young Award that year. He had won twenty-two games and had an incredible 1.12 ERA.

Gibson continued to win right up until his retirement in 1975. He was elected to the National Baseball Hall of Fame in 1981. Hall of Famer Stan Musial once summed it up best about Gibson: "Bob Gibson is a great competitor who reaches the heights he has to. . . . He's a high-class man."[2]

Bob Gibson

BORN: November 9, 1934, Omaha, Nebraska.

COLLEGE: Creighton University.

PRO: St. Louis Cardinals, 1959–1975.

HONORS: Cy Young Award in 1968 and 1970; Named MVP in 1968.
Inducted into National Baseball Hall of Fame in 1981.

In 1968, Bob Gibson led the National League with an amazing 13 shutouts and an ERA of 1.12. It was the lowest single season ERA since Dutch Leonard set the record with 1.01 in 1914.

WALTER JOHNSON

IT WAS A ROUGH TRAIN ride for Walter Johnson from New York to Washington. In 1924, at the age of thirty-six, Johnson finally had a chance to play in a World Series. But he no longer had his best stuff. Johnson had already lost two games in the 1924 World Series. He sat on the train sad and in tears about his two losses. Because of Johnson's loss in Game 5, the New York Giants were one game away from winning the World Series.

But the Washington Senators came back to win Game 6. There was one more game to play. Game 7 would decide who would win the World Championship. In that game, the Giants took a 3–1 lead, then Washington scored twice in the eighth inning to tie the score. That's when Johnson was called upon by manager Bucky Harris to keep the score tied. Johnson got the first batter out but then Frankie Frisch hit a ball off the wall for a triple.

The next player was intentionally walked. Then Johnson got tough. He knew he still had enough on his fastball to strike out George Kelly. The Washington crowd roared after Kelly struck out. They cheered even louder when Johnson retired Irish Meusel on a ground ball to end the inning.

Johnson had succeeded in keeping the score tied and the game went into extra innings. Johnson continued to battle out of trouble. In the tenth. Then in the eleventh. And again in the twelfth. The crowd roared louder each time, showing their love for this old-time warrior. Then teammate Earl McNeely rewarded Johnson's effort by singling home the winning run. Washington and Johnson had won their first World Championship. "The good Lord just couldn't bear to

Walter Johnson was always prepared for a new season. In his career, he threw seven shutouts on opening days.

see a fine fellow like Walter Johnson lose again," teammate Jack Bentley said.[1]

Walter Johnson was a fine fellow, but he was always considered a great competitor. Born on November 6, 1887, near Humbolt, Kansas, Johnson grew up on a farm in Oklahoma. His family moved to California as Walter entered high school. It was there he started to play baseball. Even at a young age, there was a good-natured side to Johnson. When his team was way ahead, he would ease up on young players or poor hitters. Johnson wanted to win all the time, but he was also a deeply sensitive man who wanted everybody to have fun at the game of baseball.

Johnson did have fun. He won 416 games, second only to Cy Young's incredible record of 511 wins. No pitcher in the American League has approached his record of winning twenty or more games in twelve different seasons. For eight straight years he led the American League in strikeouts. In 1913, Johnson didn't allow a run for fifty-six consecutive innings.

Johnson, who was elected into the National Baseball Hall of Fame in 1936, holds baseball's record for shutouts in a career—110.

Not only was Johnson a great pitcher but he was a rare individual in the early 1900s. He never drank alcohol or smoked. Johnson was just a shy, modest country boy from an Oklahoma farm who happened to throw a fastball.

"Walter Johnson was the greatest pitcher who ever lived," said Hall of Famer "Smokey" Joe Wood, who was also considered one of baseball's great pitchers.[2]

WALTER JOHNSON

BORN: November 6, 1887, Humbolt, Kansas.

DIED: December 10, 1946, Washington, D.C.

PRO: Washington Senators, 1907–1927.

RECORDS: Major League record with 110 shutouts. Pitched 56 scoreless innings in 1913.

HONORS: Elected to National Baseball Hall of Fame in 1936.

Walter Johnson won two early versions of the Most Valuable Player Award—the Chalmers Award in 1913 and the League Award in 1924.

SANDY KOUFAX

Sandy Koufax's record-breaking fourth no-hitter was a perfect game. Not a single batter reached base.

SANDY KOUFAX WAS NERVOUS. THE young Los Angeles Dodger pitcher was pitching in the 1963 World Series against the powerful New York Yankees. Koufax had grown up in Brooklyn. He knew how Yankee players like Mickey Mantle and Roger Maris could hit a baseball. After all, just a couple of years before, both Mantle and Maris had battled to break Babe Ruth's home-run record.

Roger Maris stepped up to the plate. Two years before he had hit 61 homers. Should Koufax challenge Maris with his best pitch, the fastball? Maris indeed was a great fastball hitter. Koufax received the fastball sign from his catcher and threw. "Strike one," the umpire screamed over the roar of the Dodgers fans.

Should Koufax gamble and try to surprise Maris with another fastball? Not even Babe Ruth had hit as many homers in a season as Maris had in 1961! Koufax nodded at the fastball sign and went into his windup. The ball sped past Maris on the inside corner of the plate. "Strike two," the umpire yelled. The Dodger fans' roars got louder. It appeared that Koufax was confident in his fastball.

But Koufax was a smart pitcher. He knew that he didn't have to rely on just his fastball. His third pitch to Maris was a curveball. Maris swung and missed. Strike three! Koufax struck out fifteen Yankees in that opening game of the 1963 World Series to help the Dodgers win.

During the last four seasons of his twelve-year major-league career, Koufax was the most dominant pitcher in baseball. He won twenty-five games in 1963, nineteen the following season, twenty-six in 1965, and twenty-seven in his last season.

Koufax also pitched four no-hitters and won the Cy Young Award in 1963, 1965, and 1966. He was named the Most Valuable Player of the National League in 1963. In 1965, he established a league record of strikeouts—382.

Born in Brooklyn in 1935, Sanford Koufax was a basketball star at Lafayette High School during the 1940s. His family and friends believed that he would become a professional basketball player. But Koufax loved playing the game of baseball. He made the decision to become a professional baseball player, but becoming one wasn't easy. In fact, before Koufax tried out for the Dodgers, he had failed on three previous tryouts with other major league teams. But Koufax never quit and the Dodgers believed in him. It paid off for both of them!

Koufax won 165 games and struck out more than one batter per inning before stunning the baseball world when he retired at the young age of thirty. The chronic arthritis in his left elbow would have become worse if he had continued his baseball career.

Koufax became the youngest man ever to be inducted into the National Baseball Hall of Fame in 1972. He was thirty-six. For a boy who never planned on becoming a baseball player and who was told three times that he wasn't good enough, Sandy Koufax was baseball's best pitcher of the 1960s.

The late great manager of the New York Yankees, Casey Stengel, put it all in perspective after seeing Sandy Koufax pitch. "The kid is probably the best of them all."[1]

BORN: December 30, 1935, Brooklyn, New York.

COLLEGE: University of Cincinnati.

PRO: Brooklyn (later Los Angeles) Dodgers, 1955–1966.

RECORDS: Pitched four no-hitters.

> NL record for strikeouts (382) in a season, 1965.

HONORS: National League MVP, 1963; Cy Young Award, 1963, 1965,

> 1966. Elected to National Baseball Hall of Fame in 1972.

In 1963, Koufax was named the Most Valuable Player in the National League.

CHRISTY MATHEWSON

When the National Baseball Hall of Fame was founded in 1936, Christy Mathewson was one of the first five players chosen.

CHRISTY MATHEWSON

IT WAS A WORLD SERIES that no other pitcher had ever had. Christy Mathewson was on the verge of making World Series history. He had already pitched two shutouts in the 1905 World Series against the powerful Philadelphia Athletics. Could he do it again?

On October 14, Mathewson was called upon by New York Giants manager John McGraw to try and end the series. Even though the Giants had a 3–1 lead, the Athletics were a dangerous offensive team. But there was little to worry about with Mathewson on the mound. Christy didn't walk one batter and didn't allow a runner to get past third base! The Giants won the series in five games because of Mathewson's three shutout wins.

Christopher Mathewson first learned to throw a baseball in his hometown of Factoryville, Pennsylvania, where he was born in 1880. He was the grandson of a Civil War hero and had great pride in his country. Christy, a very shy, quiet boy, developed his arm like so many youngsters in the nineteenth century—by throwing objects against the side of a barn.

Mathewson was not only developing into a fine pitcher in the late 1890s but was well educated. Very few ballplayers ever attended a university or college back then, but Christy Mathewson attended Bucknell College in 1898. He was the class president that year.

He also had unique morals for back then. He did not join his teammates when they would go out drinking and fighting. Many times Mathewson would be seen in a hotel lobby reading a newspaper or a book. He even refused to pitch on

Sundays. However, Mathewson was a great pitcher the other six days of the week.

Mathewson got his big chance when he was traded by the Cincinnati Reds to the Giants in 1900. He pitched seventeen years for the Giants. He also helped the Giants win five National League pennants and one World Series championship. Mathewson shares the National League most-wins record—373—with Grover Cleveland Alexander.

Mathewson was also one of baseball's greatest control pitchers. Rarely did he walk a batter. In fact, he once went sixty-eight consecutive innings without walking a batter! He also could strike out a batter. During his career, Christy struck out 2,502 batters.

He had control and an educated approach to the game. He added to these winning aspects by mastering the screwball pitch. Very few pitchers had ever even heard of this pitch.

This great pitcher retired from baseball in 1916 after being traded back to the Cincinnati Reds at the age of 36. After pitching all those innings, Mathewson's arm was tired and sore. Also, World War I was just starting and Mathewson wanted to help his country. So he put down his glove and went off to help defend the United States. Mathewson fought with the U.S. Army in Europe and returned home to be a coach for the Giants. But because of the poisonous chemicals Mathewson breathed in during the war, he died in 1925 at age forty-five.

Christy Mathewson was inducted into the National Baseball Hall of Fame in 1936. He is remembered as more than a great pitcher. "He was class," Giants manager John McGraw said. "He was a kind, educated man who saw more to life than baseball."[1]

CHRISTY MATHEWSON

BORN: August 12, 1880, Factoryville, Pennsylvania.

DIED: October 7, 1925, Boston, Massachusetts.

PRO: New York Giants, 1900–1916; Cincinnati Reds, 1916.

COLLEGE: Bucknell College.

RECORDS: Won 37 games in 1908.

Won 30 or more games four times.

Led the National League in strikeouts five times.

HONORS: First pitcher to be elected to National Baseball Hall of Fame, 1936.

In the 1905 World Series, Mathewson helped the New York Giants whip the Philadelphia Athletics by pitching three shutouts. In 1904, the National League Champion Giants refused to play the Boston Red Sox, the American League Champions, so no World Series was held.

SATCHEL PAIGE

Satchel Paige was a star in the Negro leagues from 1924 to 1948. By the time he entered major league baseball in 1948, he was already past his prime.

SATCHEL PAIGE

JUSTICE FINALLY CAUGHT UP TO Satchel Paige. Kept out of the major leagues because he was black, Paige became baseball's oldest rookie when he pitched for the Cleveland Indians at the age of forty-two in 1948. A crowd of 51,013 was on hand August 13 at Comiskey Park in Chicago to see the "rookie" in his first major-league start. Satchel Paige didn't disappoint the crowd. He pitched a five-hit shutout in his 5–0 victory over the White Sox. "I had my 'be-ball' working today," Paige said after the game. "I call it my be-ball 'cause it be where I want it to be."[1]

Paige made it sound simple. It wasn't. Ask any pitcher. But this remarkable athlete was always up for a challenge even at an early age. Born Leroy Paige in Mobile, Alabama, in 1906, Satchel learned about the game of baseball when he was a youngster. He often spent nights on the ball fields throwing the ball around. The young Paige dreamed about playing major-league baseball. In the 1920s, however, African Americans were not allowed to play in the major leagues. But Paige did play professional ball—in the Negro leagues. It was there that he forged his reputation as one of baseball's greatest pitchers. He pitched over 2,000 games in the Negro leagues and recorded over 250 shutouts, including 45 no-hitters.

Paige's efforts to get into the major leagues were finally rewarded after Jackie Robinson broke the color barrier in professional baseball in 1947. Paige was signed by Indians owner Bill Veeck in 1948 to give the team needed pitching help. Paige won six games, lost only one, and had one save, with a 2.48 ERA. Despite being forty-two years old, Paige was a valuable addition to the Indians. That year he became the first black pitcher to make an appearance in a World Series.

Paige continued to ignore Father Time. He had his best year in the majors when he was forty-six. That year, Paige won twelve games, eight of them in relief. He also saved ten games with a 3.07 ERA. He was selected by Yankees manager Casey Stengel to the All-Star Game that year.

After he left the major leagues, Satchel Paige played for the St. Louis Browns from 1951 to 1953. But he was back in 1965. That year, when he was *59*, Paige pitched three shutout innings for the Kansas City Athletics against the Boston Red Sox in an American League regular season game! Satchel allowed just one hit in those three innings and didn't walk one batter. Not bad for an older man!

Paige was a kind and patient man. He had the perfect attitude to be a coach. After finally retiring, he devoted some of his time to teaching young pitchers. He was an Atlanta Braves coach in 1968 and 1969. Paige's advice seemed to help. The Braves won the Western Division in 1969 but lost to the New York Mets for the right to go to the World Series that year.

Satchel Paige's accomplishments in both the Negro leagues and the major leagues were recognized in 1971 when he was inducted into the National Baseball Hall of Fame. Not bad for a man who started out as a porter at a train station in Alabama.

BORN: July 7, 1906, Mobile, Alabama.

DIED: June 8, 1982, Kansas City, Missouri.

PRO: Played in Negro leagues from 1924 to 1948 and 1951 to 1953. Pitched 45 no-hitters, over 250 shutouts, and appeared in over 2,500 games in the Negro leagues. Cleveland Indians, 1948–1949.

RECORDS: Oldest rookie in major-league history in 1948 when he signed with the Cleveland Indians.

First black player to pitch in a World Series game, 1948.

HONORS: Elected to National Baseball Hall of Fame in 1971.

Though Paige spent his best years in the Negro leagues, he did face major league batters in exhibition games. Joe DiMaggio called him the greatest pitcher he ever faced.

NOLAN RYAN

Nolan Ryan's record for strikeouts, 5,714, may never be broken. Steve Carlton is second in career strikeouts with 4,136.

NOLAN RYAN

"THE EXPRESS" WAS ROARING ONCE again in the Houston Astrodome. It was September 26, 1981. Houston Astros pitcher Nolan Ryan faced the Los Angeles Dodgers in a critical National League West battle on that Saturday afternoon. It was such a big game that the contest was being seen by millions of Americans on national television. For eight innings, Ryan had not allowed a Dodger to get a base hit. He was one inning away from breaking Sandy Koufax's major-league record of four no-hitters.

Pinch hitter Reggie Smith was the first batter up in the ninth. The crowd at the Astrodome was already on their feet. "Strrrike one," the umpire roared. Smith swung and missed for strike two. Ryan's next pitch was a high fastball. Smith swung and missed. One out!

Ryan then fell behind with a three-balls and one-strike count on Ken Landreaux. He decided to challenge Landreaux with a fastball. Ryan won! Landreaux grounded out to first base. Two outs! One to go! Dusty Baker stepped in against Ryan. Baker was a good fastball hitter, so Ryan threw only curves to him. On the fourth curve ball, Baker grounded the ball to third baseman Art Howe. The Astrodome became quiet. Howe's throw to first base was in time. A no-hitter, Ryan's fifth. Koufax's record was broken!

The crowd roared as Ryan's Astros teammates lifted him on their shoulders. Nolan Ryan was baseball's no-hit king. This type of performance had become expected of Ryan. And why not? The future Hall of Famer struck out 5,714 batters in his career. No other pitcher in baseball history can match that record.

Ryan's explosive fastball is one reason why he holds the major league record for strikeouts. It has been clocked at 100.8 miles per hour. This achievement won Ryan a place in the *Guinness Book of World Records*. Pretty good for a lad who dreamed of playing basketball when he was growing up in his hometown of Alvin, Texas. "I was always throwing something or other all the time," Ryan said. "My mother was constantly on me about breaking windows. I was successful but not superior to the other kids. I could always throw farther than the other kids—not harder, just farther.[1]

Ryan, the youngest of six children, was born in Refugio, Texas, on January 31, 1947. As a boy, he developed strong wrists by tying up newspapers quickly. He would roll 670 papers in just under five minutes.

Ryan finished out his brilliant career by playing for the Texas Rangers in 1993. It was a year that was filled with injuries for him. However, he will go down in history as "Baseball's Miracle." He threw as well at the age of forty-six as he did at nineteen. Nolan Ryan will certainly be inducted into the National Baseball Hall of Fame in the near future.

"Nolan Ryan was the only pitcher I was ever scared to face," Hall of Famer Reggie Jackson once said.[2]

NOLAN RYAN

BORN: January 31, 1947, Refugio, Texas.

PRO: New York Mets, 1968–1971; California Angels, 1972-1979;
     Houston Astros, 1980-1988; Texas Rangers, 1989-1993.

RECORDS: Pitched 7 no-hitters.

     Baseball's all-time strikeout king, 5,714.

Nolan Ryan, the pitcher with the most no-hitters, the most strikeouts, and the fastest fast ball ever recorded, was never honored with a Cy Young Award.

Tom Seaver

Only 14,197 Fans Showed Up that cold April afternoon at Shea Stadium in 1970. But what an afternoon! Tom Seaver, who had led the Mets to a World Series victory in 1969 over the powerful Baltimore Orioles, was in better than average form. And that was awesome!

By the seventh inning the fans could sense something special was happening. Seaver was nursing a 2–1 lead over the San Diego Padres. He struck out the side in the seventh and eighth innings to break a Mets record for strikeouts in a game—16. The record initially was held by Nolan Ryan. In addition, Seaver had struck out the last seven Padres!

Seaver was going for the major-league record of 8 consecutive strikeouts. Only four pitchers had ever accomplished that feat. The crowd got louder as Seaver took the mound. They screamed when "Tom Terrific" struck out Van Kelly to start the ninth inning. Could Seaver get the record? Of course! Seaver threw a fastball past Clarence Gaston for victim number eighteen and his ninth straight strikeout.

Now, Seaver was only one strikeout away from tying the then major-league record of 19 strikeouts in a nine-inning game held by Steve Carlton. Al Ferrara was the batter. Seaver's first pitch was a slider. "Strike one," yelled home plate umpire Harry Wendelstedt. The second pitch was a ball and the crowd booed the call. Seaver's next pitch was a fastball. Ferrara swung and missed for strike two! The crowd was on its feet screaming. Seaver threw a fastball again. Strike three! Seaver tied the record and set a major-league record for consecutive strikeouts—10!

TOM SEAVER

Tom Seaver was part of the lineup of the miraculous 1969 New York Mets. Against all odds, this fledgling team won their first World Series under the leadership of the legendary Gil Hodges.

"I was close and I wanted it," Seaver said after the game. "I just let the fastball rip."[1]

It was a game that sticks out in the minds of many baseball fans when talking about Tom Seaver. The pitcher was born on November 17, 1944, in Fresno, California. When he was growing up in California, Seaver was never known for having a great fastball and he was not the best pitcher in high school. The skill was something that developed over his college years at Fresno City College and at the University of Southern California.

In 1966 Seaver was offered $40,000 by the Atlanta Braves, but the contract was canceled by Baseball Commissioner William Eckert because Seaver had already begun participating with USC. He was awarded to the New York Mets in a lottery. It didn't take long before he had an impact with the Mets.

Seaver was named Rookie of the Year in 1967 after winning sixteen games. In 1969, he was 25–7 and won the Cy Young Award. He won it again in 1973. That year he won nineteen games and led the Mets to the World Series. Seaver won his third Cy Young in 1975.

Seaver was traded to the Cincinnati Reds in 1977, which caused an uproar by Mets fans. But that didn't stop him from winning. He won seventy-five games in five seasons with the Reds. He also had pitching stints with the Chicago White Sox and Boston Red Sox. He won his 300th game pitching as a White Sox against the New York Yankees in New York.

"Tom Terrific's" record is terrific. He won 60 percent of his games, compiling a 311–205 record. Seaver also struck out 3,640 batters. He was inducted into the National Baseball Hall of Fame in 1992. "Tom Seaver is the best pitcher who ever pitched," former New York Mets pitching coach Rube Walker said. "And that includes Sandy Koufax or anyone else."[2]

TOM SEAVER

BORN: November 17, 1944, Fresno, California.

COLLEGE: Fresno City College; University of Southern California.

PRO: New York Mets, 1967–1977, 1983; Cincinnati Reds, 1977–1982; Chicago White Sox, 1984–1986; Boston Red Sox, 1986.

HONORS: Named Rookie of the Year in 1967. Won Cy Young Award in 1969, 1973, 1975. Elected into the National Baseball Hall of Fame in 1992.

Seaver's greatest years were spent with the New York Mets, where he was given the Cy Young Award three times. He pitched his last year before retiring in Boston.

CY YOUNG

Between 1890 and 1911, Cy Young pitched a record 753 complete games and won a record 511 games. It's no wonder major league baseball's award for pitching excellence is named for him.

WHIZZZ! THUMP! WHIZZZ! THUMP! PEOPLE stopped and stared. A young Cleveland Spiders pitcher by the name of Denton True Young was warming up against a wooden outfield fence. Whizzz! Thump! One fan shouted out, "Look at the fence. It looks like a cyclone hit it!" The wooden fence was splintered and torn apart from Young's blazing fastball. "It does look like a cyclone," a local sportswriter agreed. "Just call him Cy, short for cyclone."[1]

The nickname and the legend began that day in 1890. Cy Young's career ended in 1911, but an award honoring pitching excellence was named after him many years later. There were plenty of reasons to honor Cy Young's memory.

Many point to a cool May day in 1909 in Boston when Young set a standard for all pitchers in modern baseball history. On that day, thirty-seven-year-old Cy Young pitched the first perfect game in this century. Up until then, only two perfect games had ever been pitched, both in the nineteenth century.

Young is baseball's all-time winning pitcher. He won an astounding 511 games! No other pitcher has come close to that record. (Walter Johnson is a distant second with 416 wins.) That's not bad for a country boy who was born on a farm in Gilmore, Ohio.

Young won at least nineteen games a year for fourteen straight years. He also set a record back then by pitching forty-four straight innings without giving up a run. That record was broken, but Young's record of 753 complete games still remains.

"The winningest pitcher in baseball history," remarked former Baltimore Orioles manager Earl Weaver about Young. "Cy Young topped the 20-victory mark in 16 different seasons and exceeded the 30-win plateau five times. It is fitting that pitching excellence is honored with an award named after him."[2]

Young was not only a great pitcher but he could handle the bat, too. During his career, Cy belted 18 home runs and had a total of 623 hits. His average was .210. Very few pitchers ever hit over .200.

When he retired, Young headed back to his farm in Peoli, Ohio. But he wasn't finished with the game of baseball. He was elected to the National Baseball Hall of Fame in 1937.

When Little League baseball began to surface in 1949, Young became interested in helping promote the organization. "Get the kids equipment, uniforms, and bats and balls," Young said. "Even if the kids you sponsor are only ten years old, get a program for them that will make them hustle every minute."[3]

Young dedicated the rest of his life to Little League baseball. He threw out the first ball at the 1955 Little League World Series. One month later, Cy Young passed away.

CY YOUNG

BORN: March 29, 1867, Gilmore, Ohio.

DIED: November 4, 1955, Peoli, Ohio.

PRO: 1890–1911: Cleveland Spiders, St. Louis Nationals, Boston Red Sox, Cleveland Indians, and Boston Braves.

RECORDS: Major League record for wins, 511.

HONORS: Award for pitching excellence was named after him. Elected to National Baseball Hall of Fame, 1937.

In 1937, Young was named to the National Baseball Hall of Fame.

NOTES BY CHAPTER

Introduction
1. Dick Belsky, *Tom Seaver—Baseball's Superstar* (New York: Henry Z. Walck, Inc., 1977), p. 8.

Grover Cleveland Alexander
1. "Baseball's 50 Greatest Games," *The Sporting News* (1986) pp. 67–68.

Roger Clemens
1. Interview with Mike Sullivan (United Press International), Yankee Stadium, Bronx, New York, June 1988.

Bob Gibson
1. Bob Gibson, with Phil Pepe, *From Ghetto to Glory* (New York: Prentice-Hall, 1970), p. 190.
2. Ibid., p. 204.

Walter Johnson
1. Jack Kavanagh, *Baseball Legends—Walter Johnson* (New York: Chelsea House Publishers, 1992), p. 15.
2. Ibid., p. 35.

Sandy Koufax
1. Jim Murray, *Baseball Legends—Sandy Koufax* (New York: Chelsea House Publishers, 1991), p. 57.

Christy Mathewson
1. *Greatest Baseball Players of All Time* (Lincolnwood, Ill.: Publications International, 1990), p. 360.

Satchel Paige
1. S. A. Kramer, *Baseball's Greatest Pitchers* (New York: Random House, 1992), p. 28.

Nolan Ryan

1. Ken Rappoport, *Nolan Ryan, The Ryan Express* (New York: Dillon, 1992), p. 13.

2. Ibid., p. 9.

Tom Seaver

1. "Baseball's 50 Greatest Games," *The Sporting News* (1986), p. 175.

2. Dick Belsky, *Tom Seaver—Baseball's Superstar* (New York: Henry Z. Walck, Inc., 1977), p. 6.

Cy Young

1. Norman L. Macht, *Baseball Legends—Cy Young* (New York: Chelsea House Publishers, 1992), p. 18.

2. Ibid., p. 65.

3. Ibid., p. 56.

INDEX